LOST
BARROW-IN-FURNESS

GILL JEPSON

AMBERLEY

Dedicated to Peter Bleasdale, a dear uncle 'lost' to us 2019.

First published 2019

Amberley Publishing
The Hill, Stroud
Gloucestershire, GL5 4EP

www.amberley-books.com

British Library Cataloguing in Publication Data.

A catalogue record for this book is available from the British Library.

ISBN 978 1 4456 9067 4 (print)
ISBN 978 1 4456 9068 1 (ebook)

Origination by Amberley Publishing.
Printed in the UK.

Contents

Introduction   4

1   A Green and Pleasant Land: The Rural Life   5

2   The Working Day: Industrial Change   20

3   Transport: Getting About   30

4   Body, Soul and Mind   41

5   Leisure   53

6   Let Me Entertain You   64

7   Shopping   72

8   Furness Abbey, Abbotswood and Furness Abbey Hotel   87

    Acknowledgements   96

Introduction

Barrow-in-Furness is a purpose-built and planned nineteenth-century town, emerging from a small village into a thriving industrial centre in just forty years. Despite the existing town centre being relatively young, the changes over the intervening years have been notable. The area has been a settlement since early history and its power bases have shifted and altered to accommodate the growing needs of the population. This book explores some of the changes and looks on the inevitable nature of this, sometimes with regret and sometimes with nostalgia. From being a rural area originally governed by the important and powerful Cistercian abbey of St Mary of Furness blossoming into a Victorian industrial town, Barrow has always risen to the challenge and adapted.

Lost Barrow-in-Furness demonstrates how much a place can change over time and how different ways of life can disappear. Nostalgia is a growth industry these days, probably because life is changing with such rapidity and we feel it's an unstoppable force. Many of the pastimes and occupations previously enjoyed have vanished and certainly the freedoms children had in the past have gone. We look back fondly and many of these pictures and words will evoke sentimental and nostalgic thoughts. However, nothing can remain static and life is change, so we must learn to embrace and accept as well as look back with more realism. The 'good old days' make us feel warm and fuzzy, but this attitude does us a disservice; we must look at the reasons for change and the natural alteration that occurs through time.

One of the key areas of change is in the central town itself. The shopping street is in massive decline and is a topic of discussion and political debate. It is too easy to blame the eponymous 'council' for decline and to use the dilapidation as the fault of one political faction or another. In reality, it is typical of most 'post-industrial' towns across the country and trying to retain a thriving commercial centre is like Canute trying to drive back the waves. I class Barrow as 'post-industrial' because although presently it still retains the shipbuilding industry, this is a boom or bust employer and Barrow has had lean times as well as prosperous ones. Its previous position as an industrial centre has depleted and its glory days are sadly over. The fortune of the town centre and shops on offer are part of this and it is not an attractive prospect for new business, which then impacts on the workforce coming to the town. Many commute or lodge rather than buying and settling, a different prospect to when the town was new and had plenty to offer.

Great efforts have been made to improve the town, but it cannot stem the flow of shoppers to the huge supermarkets on the outskirts or reduce the online culture of younger shoppers. The Barrow market is reinventing itself into a vibrant shopping venue, but it is fighting against the tide and requires more shoppers from outside the town, which is a limited pool these days.

The photographs and words reflect a time gone by and allows us to explore the places and people who make Barrow special. The photographs are gathered from personal collections and archives and provide a glimpse into some unique places – the town, the rural environment, the park, the beaches and theatres to name but a few.

A Green and Pleasant Land: The Rural Life

Barrow-in-Furness began like most places, as a collection of rural communities. Until 1845 the place we know as Barrow existed only as a tiny hamlet of some 200 souls. The settlement had the usual facilities we would expect in the nineteenth century: an inn, a blacksmith, a boat yard, a shop or two and farms and small cottages.

It had dipped its toes into the Industrial Revolution cautiously, having a range of piers to enable the shipment of slate quarried at Kirkby. The Duke of Buccleuch owned the quarry and slate was delivered to Barrow on horse-drawn wagons and then transported on boats from the piers. Iron ore was transported in the same way and this developed further when a rich seam of haematite was discovered in 1850 after years of searching. Iron ore had been mined since the time of the monks, but on a small scale. We see them exploiting the ore pits given by Roger de Orgrave, near Tytup Hall, Dalton. However, speculators descended on the area in 1839 the industry was opened. H. W. Schneider had a ready workforce from his failing tin mines in Cornwall and these people formed the backbone of the mining industry.

The site of Barrow village from the Town Hall clock. (Courtesy of Barrow Archives)

Schneider Square, close to the site of Fisher's Farm.

This was the start. The railway was to arrive next, and the Furness Railway was primed to improve the transport system. Once the final piece was in place Barrow was ready to move into the industrial age. The peninsula is a rich agricultural area and there are still many farms around the area. However, the rural life was about to change and the evidence of one of those farms is firmly in the historical record. William Fisher's farm was approximately at the top of Dalton Road, close to Schneider Square. A few fragmentary sandstone and pebble walls remain but would be unnoticed by most passers-by. William was a yeoman farmer who had substantial landholdings. He is especially interesting because he left a diary that was written at the time of the biggest changes in Barrow. He not only writes about his sowing record and animal husbandry, but he includes the local 'hatches, matches and dispatches' and gossip, giving us a colourful glimpse of early Barrow. Later we read about the huge changes implemented by the new town fathers – Ramsden, Buccleuch, Devonshire and Schneider – and the impact it had on the community.

Other early residents whose lives were changed dramatically at this time were the Michaelson family of 'old Barrow' or Barrow Island as it is now known. In the early 1840s it was a true island, seated between mainland Barrow and Walney Island. It was agricultural land as can be seen on the field map. The manor house dominated it, as depicted by Mrs Michaelson in her painting. Access to the island was by a ford at low tide and it must have presented a rural idyll.

There was a farm, which is remembered now by 'Farm Street'. It has virtually gone apart from the older buildings, which were once stables for the farm. St Patrick's presbytery was the farmhouse when the Michaelson's owned it, which had stables and a few small cottages for the workforce but little else. The remaining land was given to

Barrow Island from a painting by Mrs Michaelson.

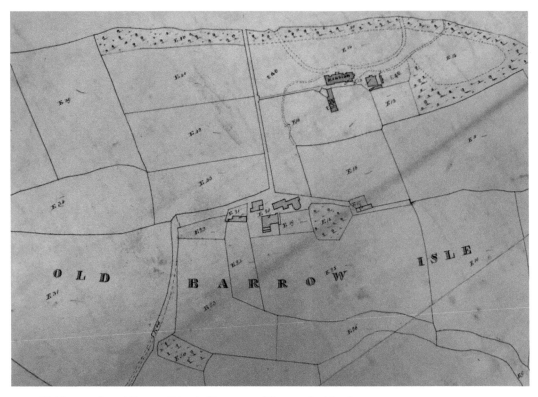

Field map of rural Barrow Island. (Courtesy of Barrow Archives)

Site of the Michaelson's farm, now the St Patrick's presbytery.

The original farmhouse, which became the presbytery.

agricultural use, planting and orchards. It was a prime piece of real estate and when Mr Thomas Yeates Parker Michaelson died his wife sold it lock, stock and barrel to Furness Shipbuilding Company. This enabled the company to expand and develop a proper shipyard and dock system. The island nowadays is only discernible as an island by the two bridges one crosses to access it from Michaelson Road or at the other side at Jubilee Bridge from Walney. The land is covered by huge construction sheds and Victorian engineering workshops. Nowadays we find a school, a church and multiple housing developments, some of which originally provided the shipyard workers' accommodation close to work and recycled their wages back to the employer through their rent.

Barrow Island is a mixture of industry, housing and wasteland with a variety of itinerant buildings now derelict. It leads to the Ramsden Dock, which was one of four constructed between 1872 and 1879. While it does not have the same capacity as when steel was being shipped through the port, it still handles shipments of local limestone, granite, sand and aggregates and is a berth for the BNFL ships handling nuclear waste. It has changed its purpose with the advent of the gas terminals at Rampside and more recently has been a base for supplying the wind turbines in the Irish Sea, making it an important part of the renewable energy industry. Adjacent to Ramsden Dock is Cavendish Dock, which never lived up to its potential.

The change to the landscape has arisen from this change and it is now the only access to the port, which is now enclosed. This area is being marked for development. A business park and waterfront development is planned and BAE Systems, who now own the shipyard, are expanding their workforce to meet the requirements of the new

Renewed entrance to the Ramsden Dock.

Successor class submarines that are to be built in the town. Access to Barrow Island from mainland Barrow is the High-Level Bridge, which connects the town almost seamlessly, as it runs across into Michaelson Road again recalling the family. The connection to Walney is by Jubilee Bridge and the Low-Level Bridge, which connected the other side of the island, which has completely vanished.

One thing that appears to have stayed the same is the community. It is and always has been a close-knit community and despite its social issues in some areas this remains the same. Transport is now by bus and car, whereas originally there were both trams and a railway. We have a hint of the old farmland in the Crow's Nest public house, which is built close to the site of three fields – Crow Nest, Middle Crow Nest and Near Crow Nest; but who would guess looking at the area now?

At the outskirts of the town the landscape is still a rural one. Once reached by the Greengate or Barrow Lane (Abbey Road) or through Salthouse the farms at the edge of town melt around the urban buildings. Greengate is no longer green and cuts through terraced housing and a dense council estate. It arrives on Friars Lane, which would have probably led to Salthouse farms, an ancient settlement dating to monastic times when the monks harvested salt from the marshes. In the other direction is Roose. Roose Farm is now a private house surrounded by houses, but Roosecote is still a working farm in the real sense. In this area fields and farmland stretch to the coast and have been farmed for centuries. One can see the intrusion of mining, especially at Yarlside and Stank, the workings now abandoned and covered with grass once more and grazing sheep. Many of these will have started out as granges belonging to the monks at Furness Abbey.

Michaelson Road Bridge.

Location of the Low-Level Bridge.

The Crow's Nest public house.

Some of the early abbey granges still exist as farms, such as Roosecote, Parkhouse and Manor Farm. Land use is the same, but the ways in which its managed has changed. Roosecote was a sheep farm and would have been a profitable enterprise for the monks. Farms have had to diversify into other areas, such as wood dealing, land rental, dairy farming, holiday accommodation or supporting technology such as turbines, mobile masts and as at Roanhead farm a solar farm. The farmland was disturbed by industry and mining, but much of it has reverted to its original purpose along side these new ventures. The biggest threat to the agricultural landscape is housing development and fields are being sold piecemeal and the last vestiges of greenbelt are being ravaged and destroyed.

Parkhouse Farm is a successful and thriving farm with livestock and a wood yard. They developed farmland and buildings to provide bespoke housing, presumably to build their economy. They have acquired much of the land around Furness Abbey and are a large concern. Manor Farm have livestock and have reduced their holdings over the years, selling for various developments close by. This farm is very close to the abbey and a local protest ensued against plans to build houses on a field adjacent to the West Gate. The plans were turned down on appeal and the small green barrier between the busy urban landscape and the medieval heritage landscape was saved. Everywhere one looks is pasture and managed agricultural land. We tend to gaze on this sentimentally and imagine it to be natural, when in fact it is sculpted by human hands over many centuries to gain the land's rich resources. Of course, it is desirable and important to protect the landscape and natural environment from intrusive or unsympathetic developments that encroach on this vital asset, but it is becoming very difficult to fight powerful developers.

Grazing land at Dungeon Lane, Roosecote Farm.

Parkhouse Farm, an abbey grange and surrounding countryside.

A real candidate for 'Lost Barrow' is the vanished medieval village of Sellergarth, which was located close to the abbey and possibly near where the current Manor Farm stands now. The story goes that Abbot Alexander Banke, an unpopular man, wanted to seize the land to create a larger deer park for hunting in. He had already acquired various farms like Roose, Sandscale, Goldmire, Southend and Roanhead to create park land for deer. He was expelled by a faction of monks and some villagers of Sellergarth, but returned two years later and exacted his revenge. He decided that Sellergarth would add to his deer park and he despatched twenty-two monks with cudgels in December to evict the villagers. The village was destroyed and the tenants turned out. The action was illegal and defied Henry VII's statute 'against pullyng doun of Tounes' and Henry VIII's statute stating that 'townes, villages, borowes and hamlettes, tythyng houses, and other enhabitation' where there 'was or were used and occupied to tillage and husbandrye' should not be destroyed.

In 1516, William Case and his wife, evicted tenants of Sellargarth, took Banke to court – a common experience for him by all accounts. We don't have a definitive conclusion to the story, other than the villagers probably set up homes in 'New Barns' (Newbarns), Bridge Gate, Breast-Mill Beck and Rakesmoor. The current farmer at Manor Farm is William Case's descendant, providing an ironic twist to the story. The location of the lost village is still under debate. Some scholars favour the location west of Hawcoat, near Sowerby Hall Farm. George Case, descendant of William has been recorded as saying that he believed it to be roughly where Barrow Sixth Form College is. Until some archaeological evidence is discovered, we might never know.

The ancient farms at Salthouse again date back to monastic times. The marsh area provided rushes and salt and was worked by the lay brothers from the abbey. Salt

13

was another lucrative commodity which the monks readily exploited. The farms sit incongruously among terraced streets, unremarkable at first glance. The salt ponds were used to collect the salt and then processed in open boiler pans. The area where this was done is now part of the Cavendish Dock site – some of the later derelict industrial land is being reclaimed by nature and reeds and grasses are returning.

The original houses at Salthouse were made of cobbles and mud – probably clay. Roof timbers were sourced locally, and roofs were thatched with straw. Inside, the cottages were simple with floors made from pebbles, which wore smooth and flat over time. They were primitive habitation with loft bedrooms reached by ladders. Later these were rebuilt or modified to provide better and more modern accommodation. The yeomen farmers who lived in some of these farm building worked the surrounding land until the nineteenth century. Indeed, Sir James Ramsden when he arrived in Barrow as a twenty-three-year-old railway manager lodged with the Kendalls. This house built in 1802 still exists and is a Grade II listed building.

Some of the boundary walls are old cobble and sandstone, giving a lasting clue to its ancient past. The fields and agricultural land now lie beneath mostly nineteenth-century houses, roads and the railway.

Another interesting farm that still exists as a working farm is Roanhead. This has adapted more than most but has retained its original purpose as well. It was originally located further west and was physically moved and rebuilt in its current location to accommodate the sinking of the pit head for the Nigel pit. The area around Roanhead has a distinctive landscape, forged by iron ore mining, but retaining its rich natural

Could this be the site of Sellergarth?

One of the old walls at Salthouse village looking towards the Sandgate pub.

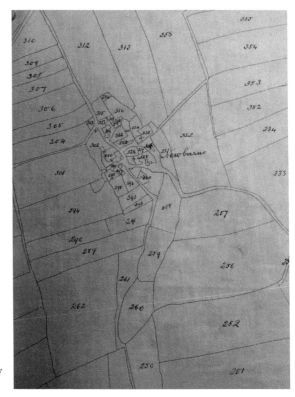

Tithe map of Salthouse village. (Courtesy of Barrow Arhcives)

Cavendish Dock, near the Sandgate.

Old Farmhouse on Salthouse Road.

heritage. The iron ore workings have gone and nature has reclaimed them, creating ponds and natural habitats for a variety of animals. Sandscale Haws, which lies beside the old workings, is a rich and diverse area with sand dunes and rare natterjack toads and many sea birds.

The farm itself embraced the new 'industry' of the age in renewable energy and developed a solar energy farm. It is an efficient producer of solar power and everything has been done to retain environmentally friendly aspects. Tree cover and vegetation on the site has been maintained and a public right of way has been preserved. Native species hedgerows and species-rich grasses have been planted to maximise the diversity, and meadow grassland is being encouraged and established. The provision of access corridors and mammal flaps enhance the area for wildlife, including deer, foxes and hares, and nesting boxes for bats and birds have been installed. Altogether a more sensitive approach than in the nineteenth-century developments.

Of course, farms have reduced in number over many years. In Barrow some disappeared as land was sold for housing, leaving farm buildings obsolete. One of these is Holbeck Farm, now almost forgotten and known now as Crofters public house. It sits incongruously among a huge estate of houses, where before it was surrounded by fields. The building, dating from 1828 retains its external integrity and it's easy to recognise the farm buildings, some of which are much earlier than the farmhouse. The cow house and barn originate from the 1700s, with surrounding walls back to 1800. Most of these have been turned into other accommodation, while the huge farmhouse is now the hostelry. It is sad that is no longer serving its original purpose, but at least it is intact as a building.

Nigel pond.

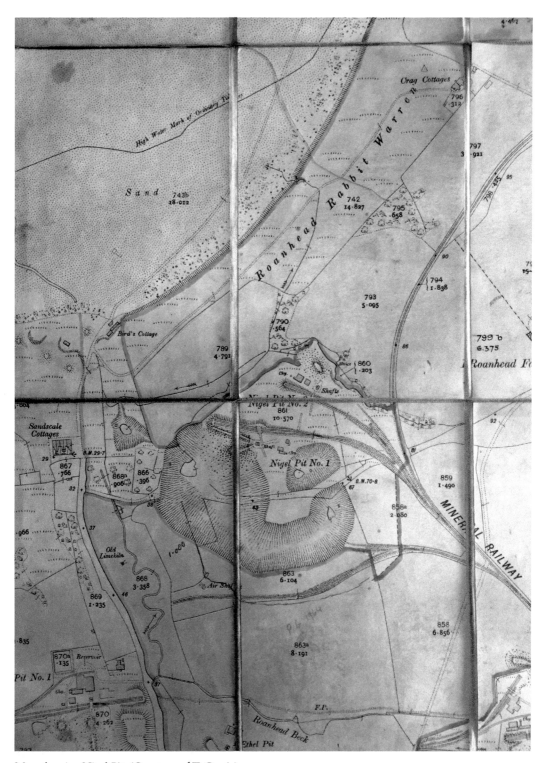

Map showing Nigel Pit. (Courtesy of T. Curtis)

Roanhead Solar Farm – rural and new industry together. (Courtesy of T. Curtis)

Holebeck Farm, now known as Crofters public house.

2

The Working Day: Industrial Change

In the early days Barrow was a small village with the trades that traditionally served such communities, such as farming, fishing, labouring and mining. The complexion of the place altered gradually, with the key driver being the development of iron ore mining from small scale to industrial. Mining had always been present and is recorded in the Coucher Books from Furness Abbey by the monks. Much of the red hematite was extracted via small open cast mines and processed locally in kilns during monastic times as archaeological evidence has shown.

The iron ore was a rich vein, but this had run its course by the First World War and the mines closed one by one. This major industry disappeared leaving only the buildings, railways and earthworks still visible in the landscape. The iron ore mines transformed the landscape while they were being worked and have left some significant scars and remnants of buildings, which would have been utilised at the time but now serve other purposes. Stank and Roose are notable for these memorials to industrial endeavour. There is evidence in Roose village of the railway embankment and the old line that took the mainly Cornish miners to work. The line is fragmented but the old bridge above it near the site of the old Roose Hospital is still in use, despite the trackway beneath being overgrown and returned partly back to nature.

Bridge over the old line at Roose.

The Yarlside, Askam and Lindal mines all present anomalies in the landscape, reminding us of the vast industrial disturbance wrought on this previously rural scene. The Yarlside mine presents a huge gaping scar where a shaft collapsed, luckily not causing any casualties. It glows red in the sunlight to this day, exposing its vivid red clay to the world.

Askam was built to support the iron and steel industry in the nineteenth century and grew up around it. The remains of the industry are clearly visible today, although frequently overlooked and forgotten. From the position of the Roanhead farmland, the old mine workings, now a water-filled pond, can be seen and looking out to the sea a pier protrudes into the water. The pier is made from iron slag and looks more natural than architectural, providing a promontory for those brave enough to walk along it.

Barrow itself retains the evidence for its past industrial history too. A huge slag bank remained after the steelworks closed its doors. The structure dominated the landscape, defining the entrance to the town. At night after tipping the mound glowed red and was a definitive landmark. The council have attempted to ameliorate the damage by reducing it in size over the years an eventually landscaping it with grass and bushes. It is still an imposing size, and now provides a place for walkers and the view over the channel is beautiful. From Walney it still presents as a grey cliff, but looks less obvious these days.

Barrow has had some remarkable and impressive structures, and many of these have now gone, being replaced by others. The shipyard has always dominated the skyline, first with cranes and now with enormous sheds like the Devonshire Dock Hall and the newer submarine construction shed. The familiar cranes disappeared one by one – the final one, an iconic yellow hammer head crane, was dismantled in 2010. This crane had

Yarlside mine.

Iron ore pond and Askam Pier.

been 'in the wars' literally, having suffered bomb damage during the Second World War. The skyline looks different now and the final crane removal heralds the end of an era.

Sometimes loss is derived from a familiar feature being removed. Barrow once bristled with cranes – testament to the extent of the work going on in the shipyard. Indeed, the large Titan Hammerhead crane became an iconic feature and was symbolic of the town's heritage. This crane was unfortunately hit by enemy fire on the night of 7–8 May 1941 and two men lost their lives while fire-watching. Thomas Cooke, the crane driver, and Christopher Fieldhouse, an apprentice fitter, were killed when the crane was damaged and brought down. Although the crane no longer stands there is a plaque to the men, which remains on the 2 metres of the metal left as a permanent memorial.

Barrow bristled with chimneys in the nineteenth century, pumping out carbon-based pollution, which we now know causes ill health and environmental damage. The iron foundries and steelworks were numerous and jostled for position by the water's edge. The industry was a large employer and the workforce lived close to them. Many people were drawn to Barrow to work in the iron and steel industry and comprised yet another group of 'immigrants' to the town. One of the key places they came from was the Black Country and the Midlands. They provided smiths and metalworkers, and they brought their families with them.

The processing and smelting of iron ore began in 1859, founded by H. W. Schneider and Robert Hannay. This became the Barrow Hematite Steel Company in 1864, with James Ramsden and Josiah Smith now involved. They brought in the innovative Bessemer Steel process, which revolutionised steel production. The supply of iron ore dried up and the steel industry declined slowly. The town changed and developed over the intervening years and chimneys and foundries became fewer, pollution less dense

Walney Channel and the old slag bank.

Iconic cranes at the shipyard. (Courtesy of Barrow Archives)

The remaining hammer head crane. (Courtesy of Barrow Archives)

STEEL WORKS. BARROW-IN-FURNESS.

Steelworks chimneys, Barrow.

Townscape showing the steelworks in the distance.

and industry had to diversify. There were some lean years and the final closure of the steelworks came in the 1980s. To the untrained eye one would hardly know these monolithic buildings ever existed, but there are clues if one cares to look.

The Victorians were keen railway enthusiasts and indeed the inception of Furness Railway was one of the catalysts for the growth of industry in Barrow. The main line diverts from its original route, and its original station lies derelict at the foot of St George's Hill. The creation of a second station moved the emphasis of the railway away from the coast. The old line that went to Rampside is disused and is now a country walk through a semi-industrial coastal area. We can find evidence of defunct lines all over Barrow. Goods and items needed for the industry in the town were moved by train and a few railway stations were dotted about. Some of these still exist, but others have been demolished or reduced in size.

The railway lines near the Corn Mill have been removed, but the retaining walls and engine sheds are still visible. A main road passes through to where the Low Road crossing was and has replaced the numerous rails. The Corn Mill was an imposing building near the Barrow waterfront built around 1871 by a syndicate of the usual businessmen and town worthies. It was steam powered and was built by William Gradwell, a local builder and businessman. After a few financial problems it changed hands twice. By 1903 Edward Hutchinson had purchased the mill from Walmsley and Smith. It was the first building in Barrow to have electric lighting and there was a sprinkler system fitted, which was extremely innovative for its time. It closed in the 1960s and was destroyed by fire in 1972. The area around the Corn Mill now supports a retail outlet for B&Q. Its existence is remembered in the name of the road: Cornmill Crossing.

We can see where lines criss-crossed the area on Barrow Island and around the shipyard. Some have only been destroyed recently, but many older residents can remember them when still in use. Island Road railway station, which also served

Railway near the Cornmill. (Courtesy of Barrow Archives)

Island Road, where the station used to stand.

Barrow Shipyard, was at the centre of the island and connected to branch lines through the town. It operated from 1899 and closed in 1967. It had principally been created for industrial use and for transporting the workforce for the yard; it had over 1,500 passengers on the workers' trains. By 1915 a second platform was added, and a public service was added for excursions, which included sports events and outings. The only evidence left is grass-covered embankments and metal posts from the platform.

The rail lines connected the shipyard with both the other industrial areas and on to Barrow Island. These lines ran adjacent to the road and went right into the shipyard, enabling delivery of goods where they were needed. The whole area must have been hectic and busy and in the early days would have been pulled by steam engines. The lines became obsolete and have now been removed in preference for the road access for large lorries.

Other industry has come and gone in Barrow and frequent attempts to diversify have not endured, unlike the shipbuilding industry. Sometimes these factories or businesses gradually bled out and became obsolete, others were relocated, and some had their end hastened by disaster or destruction. The Jute Works was an enormous building where the Range, Age UK (Lakeland House) and John Whinnerah Institute stand now. It was a mass employer of women and had been built in response to the 'frontier' town image that the new town had gained. Ramsden and others believed that an influx of females would civilise the largely male population. We don't know if this was the case, but it might have provided prospective partners at the least. There is a wonderful film of the Jute Works in 1902 of workers leaving the textile factory by Mitchell and Kenyon. The women and girls exit the works, most of them wrapped in shawls, heads covered and smiling curiously at the camera. It is a marvellous piece of social history.

Ferry Road running past the shipyard.

Two of the buildings that replaced the Jute Works have been repurposed. The Lakeland Laundry (Lakeland House) is still in use, but now houses Age UK rather than the laundry. It is externally just as it was, but inside has been modernised. The John Whinnerah Institute has fared less well. The building was demolished except for the outer façade. The building is a mere shell, surrounding newer, less attractive models, housing retail outlets.

Numerous businesses that combined to make up the local industry have now disappeared, often being replaced by retail outlets or small businesses. The heavy industry is greatly reduced and the job market in this area is less diverse. The one industry that has managed to adapt and grow is shipbuilding. The shipyard is still a major employer and thrives, having been awarded contracts for the final Astute class submarine and the new Dreadnought class. Their submarine construction sheds replace some of the old Victorian workshops and dominate the skyline.

Hindpool was particularly important for industry and it was here that William Gradwell's Hindpool Saw Mill was situated. This covered 7 acres and was where Hollywood Park is now. The wood was unloaded from the Devonshire Dock, which is now obscured by the huge Devonshire Dock Hall. Gradwell was an influential builder in Barrow and he had grown his business from small beginnings at Roose. He was responsible for many of the buildings that have survived today. His distinctive 'Gradwell' bricks can be found all over the town. Notable buildings he constructed include the Duke of Edinburgh Hotel, St James' Church, Barrow Shipbuilding Works, Barrow Steam Corn Mill, the post office and Ramsden Square. Less-illustrious projects included Crellin Street and many other terraced streets.

Ramsden Square and the Jute Works. (Courtesy of Barrow Archives)

John Whinnerah
Institute façade.

BAE Systems buildings.

Hindpool Saw Mill.

3

Transport: Getting About

Barrow's transport system has changed vastly over the years. One reason is that many people now prefer to drive, so this has reduced the amount of public transport. Furness Railway was a private company that served the public and took freight in and out of Barrow. Some of the public stations have managed to survive but others have not. Barrow is still the main station and terminus for some trains, whereas Roose and Dalton, though still there, are now unmanned and the original buildings have been reduced or demolished. The maroon and cream wooden buildings are long gone and soulless glass shelters greet the traveller these days. Local enthusiasts help to improve

Roose station before it was demolished.

Roose station entrance now.

Roose station looking west.

the look of the station by planting flowers and shrubs and shortly information panels about the area are to be installed.

Askam is very well preserved and the buildings are almost completely as they were. This station is an important one for workers travelling along the original line to service the slate quarry at Kirkby. Nowadays though their destination is likely to be Sellafield where many local people work.

A station much lamented is the Furness Abbey station, which was once a popular stop for tourists. It was opened in 1846 early in the history of Furness Railway. It later welcomed visitors from other places when the London and North Western Railway was connected to the Furness line. The abbey was the historic venue for visitors, but they were also able to take refreshments or stay at the Furness Abbey Hotel, which was owned by Furness Railway. The station was removed in 1950 and no trace remains. It was located just along from the Abbey Tavern – a glimpse of the area where the siding for Sir James Ramsden was. The line runs through the green belt from Barrow, through Roose and beyond. The abbey is revealed in all its glory as the train emerges through the tunnel and is a highlight for any traveller as it trundles past the ancient east window.

The railway additionally provided a parcel service and the original form of transport was horse drawn. The stables were on the Strand, roughly where Morrisons stands now. Later the parcel porters and delivery men were given smart vans in the company livery. The picture is of the author's grandfather with his van in the 1950s.

Of course, as popular as the railway was, it wasn't the only form of transport in Barrow. Barrow was a planned town with rectilinear streets, which mean that it was

Askam station.

The location of Furness Abbey station.

Ben Cowan Parcel Porter with his van.

ideal for a tram system. The wide, straight roads were perfect for the installation of tram lines. Barrow-in -Furness Tram Company was owned by Barrow Council and its first trams were steam powered and began in 1885. Four years later, in 1899, the trams were electrified by British Electric Traction, providing a cleaner and more modern system. The routes followed Abbey Road, Duke Street and Salthouse and Roose Road as well as a line to Barrow Island and Walney. In 1920 the Corporation took over again and this lasted until 1932 when the last tram, No. 45, made its final journey on 5 April 1932, driven by William Parsons. Trams fell out of popularity and were regarded as inefficient, slow and dirty, giving way to motor buses instead.

Motor buses were arriving as an alternative to other forms of transport in Barrow by the First World War. British Electric Traction Company applied for licences in 1915 to run a bus service from Barrow to Dalton and Ulverston. The bus service gradually overtook the trams, finally replacing them in the 1930s. Leyland buses became a familiar sight across the area, and these were adopted by Barrow Corporation Transport, distinctive in their Corporation colours of blue and cream. The buses were housed in a garage in Salthouse Road initially, in the same vicinity as the tram depot. A new depot was opened in Hindpool Road in 1936. Bus routes expanded and served most of the outlying areas of the town, some following the old tram routes. This depot was located close to where the Aldi store and car park sits now.

Tram and horse-drawn cab and taxi rank in Cavendish Square.

Barrow's first omnibuses. (Courtesy of Barrow Archives)

Following the Transport Act of 1985, the Corporation began trading as Barrow Borough Transport Limited. There was a long-running battle for custom with the Ribble bus service, which served locations beyond Barrow and Ulverston. Eventually, Barrow Borough Transport Ltd succumbed and ceased trading in 1989. Later, Ribble itself was absorbed into the much larger, national operator Stagecoach. Since then the bus service has been streamlined and routes altered to fit with the ever-changing townscape. Some routes that have fewer passengers have been reduced or even cut; this has affected outlying districts and local resistance to closure has been very strong. Some of the rural routes have been taken over by community groups or small bus companies.

Early in Barrow's history transport was principally by horse-drawn vehicles and we can see from the photographs that there was a transition from these to motorised vehicles. The smaller conveyances (like cabs) remained horse powered even after the innovation of trams and buses for some time. Horses were used on land and for hauling even though other methods were presenting themselves. Slowly, the motorised bus and car became more popular and eventually replaced the horse. This was certainly true with the transport of slate and iron ore in the 1840s: horse-drawn wagons had originally deposited the heavy goods to the jetties in Barrow. The railway took on most of this business and gradually the other methods disappeared. Motorised vehicles eventually gained importance and now we see huge lorries carrying heavy equipment in and out of the town. Some of the large components used in the shipyard

When in Barrow use the Corporation
Transport Services for visiting the various
places of interest

FREQUENT SERVICE
TO ALL PARTS

SAFE
SURE

RELIABLE
REGULAR

For Official Time Table of Transport Services apply:
General Manager, Transport Offices
Salthouse Road, Barrow-in-Furness

Advert for Corporation Buses in the 1950s.

and for the wind turbine industry are extremely large and must be escorted in by police as wide loads.

The access to Walney Island has changed markedly. A 'lost' aspect of this is the ferry, which used to be the only way to reach the island at high tide, other than by boat. Before the ferry was built there had been fords across Walney Channel as an alternative means of access. However, with industrialisation and the creation of a proper harbour many of these footways were lost. Constant dredging to allow boats into the Devonshire Dock had eradicated the old ways and the crossings near North Scale were totally removed. Furness Railway had taken ownership of the new harbour and began constructing the dock system in 1863 and caused major difficulties to the inhabitants of Walney with the removal of these access points. Walney was not originally recognised as part of the borough and came under the jurisdiction of Dalton parish. This naturally made it difficult for the residents to negotiate a solution. In 1873 a petition was raised but no solution was forthcoming. Finally, the Walney landowners demanded that Furness Railway restore the footpaths, or they would claim compensation. This ultimately did the trick and they agreed to the provision of a steam ferry as a cheaper alternative to renovating the old footpaths.

A ferry was established in 1878 and the original footings can be seen today. Its position is remembered in the name of The Ferry public house on the Walney side. There were still demands for a bridge, however, which were objected to by both the council and Furness Railway. In 1901 an offer to buy the ferry was rejected and the Furness

Horse-drawn transport on Michaelson Road Bridge. (Courtesy of Barrow Archives)

Walney Island Ferry.

Railway made a statement that no permanent crossing should be allowed unless it crossed north of the graving dock. It was at this time that Walney had been bought by Vickers Sons and Maxim and had started to build their Vickerstown estates for workers. The increase in population on Walney Island naturally demanded a better and bigger ferry to accommodate the new residents. In 1902 Vickers commissioned a rival ferry and in 1903 the old ferry was replaced too. In 1908 the bridge was finally realised, and this became the access point we know today.

Other ferries were also in use from the port of Barrow, but on a larger scale. Furness Railway, never one to miss an opportunity, recognised that workers were now looking for holidays and days away from the daily grind. Excursions became increasingly popular and people wanted new experiences. Barrow was no different and there were ferries to and from Fleetwood across Morecambe Bay from 1901. The *Lady Moyra* was one of the vessels that carried people on this exciting sea trip. Photographs of these ferry services are astonishing to the modern eye. Every available space on deck is occupied and one wonders about the safety of such overloaded vessels. The paddle steamer ships *Lady Evelyn* and *Lady Moyra* plied their trade across Morecambe Bay, but there were other steam packets that sailed to and from Barrow and there was also a service to the Isle of Man. These trips were popular until the 1960s and could be experienced as a day trip. The Isle of Man Steam Packet Company still exists but sadly no longer berths at Barrow. The novelty of travel by boat must have been in sharp contrast to the daily walk or bike ride to work, which of course was many people's preferred mode of transport.

Walney Steam Ferry.

Duke of Devonshire paddle steamer.

Lady Moyra.

4

Body, Soul and Mind

When Barrow was still a village there was no dedicated church and people had to travel to Dalton St Mary's Church, Walney Chapel or Rampside to bury their dead, marry and baptise their children. William Fisher of Barrow is known to have paid for a pew in the church at Dalton to assure a seat for his family. The village was too small to have its own parish church in the early days, but as it transformed into a small town the need for spiritual guidance was realised. The first church built was St George's, which became the parish and civic church in 1861. However, the assortment of incomers to the town demanded a greater range of places to worship. Four evangelist churches were established in 1877: St Matthew, Mark, Luke and John. These began life as temporary buildings but were rebuilt over time. St Mark's is the one original building left, with some adaptations to modernise it. St John's was completely rebuilt in 1935 in a Spanish style, using concrete construction methods.

St Luke's before demolition.

St Matthew's and St Luke's were rebuilt in the 1960s in a modern style. St Matthew's, consecrated in 1967, is lost in the sense that it no longer functions as a church. A shrinking congregation and structural issues caused the shock closure in 2017. The older church hall is functioning as a community hall and there is an ongoing consultation. The church and local people are striving to think of a way to utilise the building. St Luke's, consecrated in 1964, eventually suffered from a declining congregation, high maintenance costs and huge structural problems, which came to a head in 2008 when it closed.

A final service was held in 2012 and the building was demolished. The diocese decided that residential buildings should be built for vulnerable adults with learning difficulties on the site and Barrow Council granted planning permission unanimously. The building has now been completed and the site remembers the 'lost' church in the name of Church House. Sadly, the iconic modernist bell tower was also demolished, and one can't help thinking that it would have added a nostalgic note to the new buildings.

With the influx of workers from different places there was a need for a range of places of worship too. Religion was an important part of life for some of these people and this meant that churches had to be built. A number of churches sprung up across the town and were reflective of the populations they served. In the mostly Cornish settlement at Roose two churches were built. One was a very simple mission church called St Perran's, built in 1874 and named after the patron saint of Cornwall. It served the Anglican element of the village. Many Cornish were of the Methodist persuasion, so this entailed the building of a chapel at Stonedyke to serve them in 1877.

Church House.

The two places of worship continued over the intervening years, but as congregations shrank the chapel was abandoned and the two congregations amalgamated for expediency, sharing the St Perran's building from 1991. St Perran's had a fire in 1966 and a third little church was built and consecrated in 1967. However, this too ended when it was closed in 2014 and for the first time in 140 years Roose has no dedicated place of worship. The chapel is now derelict and in private hands and sadly St Perran's was demolished and a new house was erected on the site. The earlier church fronting Rampside Road has been demolished since the 1980s and has a private bungalow built on the site.

Other Nonconformist churches that bit the dust included Hindpool Methodist Church. This has variously been a nightclub, once known as Scorpio and more recently Skint, which seems a little ironic considering the Methodist no-alcohol pledge. It has secured its legacy by appearing in J. K. Rowling's book *Career of Evil*. It still survives, but not as it was originally intended.

Emmanuel Congregational Church situated on Ainslie Street was established in 1876. It was later extended, and it was then it became known as Emmanuel. In 1931 the Hindpool Road Congregational Church amalgamated with Emmanuel. The church became too expensive to keep in good repair and in 1991 it closed, being demolished two years later. The site was redeveloped and is now housing for the elderly and the only recognisable feature from the church is the boundary wall around the flats.

Interior of St Perran's, 2014.

New buildings on the site of St Perran's.

Emmanuel Congregational Church. (Courtesy of Barrow Archives)

It was not only Nonconformist and Anglican churches that were abandoned. The church that served the Roman Catholic community on Barrow Island, St Patrick's, is now also closed. With the influx of many Irish workers there was an immediate need to provide a Roman Catholic school and church for those of that persuasion. Many lived on Barrow Island, initially in the Barrow Island huts and later in the buildings constructed for the workers. The original chapel of ease was served by St Mary's and with the growing population a new chapel and school opened in 1885 replacing earlier temporary buildings. In 1901 the church became a separate parish and the first priest was Father Barry. At this time Walney was growing rapidly with the new Vickerstown estates and a chapel of ease was set up in 1916. The church we see now was built in 1933 and the clergy occupied the large Michaelson farmhouse and turned it into the presbytery. In 1949, St Columba became a separate parish which eventually impacted on the St Patrick's parish, becoming the dominant church. St Patrick's continued as the parish church until 2009 when it closed for the last time. The parish was combined with that of St Columba on Walney and is now known as the parish of St Columba and St Patrick.

Some losses are more poignant than others and this is certainly true of the provision for children and the disadvantaged. The old workhouse, which later became Roose Hospital, still bore the negative connotations until its demolition. The severe and foreboding building was a place to be feared, which was exactly what the town fathers

St Patrick's RC Church.

wanted to convey. Social care was more punitive than today, and it was always a last resort for those who had to use it. It opened in 1880 and dominated the surrounding landscape. Inmates were segregated according to gender and age and the idea was to promote discipline. The dehumanisation of the inmates was complete with families separated and hard labour to repay the perceived debt to society. It had vegetable gardens and a yard for stone breaking and all the usual domestic tasks were included in the work which was expected. The residents were expected to earn their bread before they received it. The harshness was embedded into the social consciousness and its reputation was set. The stigma was such that children born there were given the address '1 Rampside Road' to avoid the evidence that it was a workhouse. In 1949 it was converted to a hospital mainly for geriatric and gynaecological medicine. It closed as a hospital when Furness General Hospital opened, but continued until the early 1990s as a geriatric hospital and patients were dispersed to other establishments on closure. A housing estate has replaced the hospital, though the external wall and trees have been retained, but you would be hard pressed to realise what its original purpose was.

The remnants of other social provision have survived better than the workhouse. The Barrow Cottage Homes built in 1905 are no longer used to house children who are in need. They are still there but have been converted into private homes and the largest is now a funeral directors. They stand imposingly on Roose Road and are not unattractive. In their day they housed up to seventy-seven children. The guardians had a sensitive approach, employing a 'foster mother' for each house to enable the children to experience 'such kindness and attention as they would receive in a good home'.

North Lonsdale Hospital has long gone, the Victorian hospital that dominated the St George's site has been replaced by modern apartments and only the nurses' home

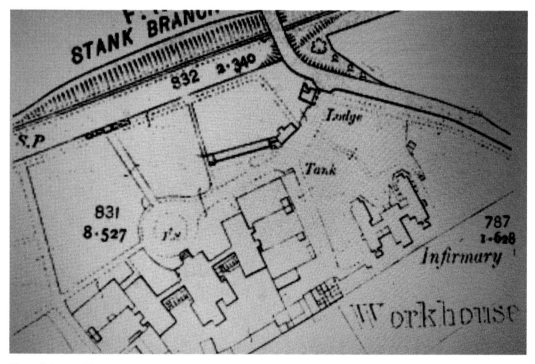

Plan of the workhouse.

Balmoral estate on the workhouse site.

The Cottage Homes.

The Cottage Homes Administrative Building.

remains on Albert Street. It was opened in 1874 and was modern and cutting edge for its time, with Nightingale wards. The hospital was run under a much stricter regime than hospitals today. Life was strictly regimented and ordered and visiting hours were minimal and properly observed. The photograph shows one of the wards, probably in the 1950s, patients neatly in their beds, crisp white sheets and nurses starched and ironed to within an inch of their lives. However, there is a glimpse of light-heartedness: the ward is decorated for Christmas and everyone is at least smiling.

The schools of the town have been reorganised, academised and many have disappeared altogether. There are significant gaps in the educational landscape and obviously replacements. We always look back with nostalgia when some of the old buildings disappear, but of course, some are just reinvented. It feels as though part of your existence is ripped away when your school is demolished, but it is often something we have no control over.

I was privileged to have a tour of my school just prior to it being demolished. It brought back many memories and it did make me sad to see the detail and style of the school knowing its parquet tiles would be ripped up and the wood panels would be broken. Sadly, mine, the Grammar School (or Parkview, as it was known later), is not the only school to be thus treated. The school was set on fire in an arson attack just prior to demolition. There is now a housing estate under construction.

Some of the older schools have gone, such as Thwaite Street School, which was built in 1887. It was the usual Victorian style with classrooms branching off the hall. The

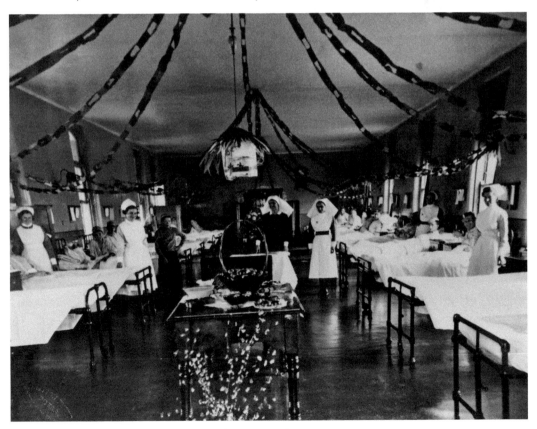

North Lonsdale Hospital. (Courtesy of Barrow Archives)

photograph is of the infants Christmas pageant – taken in 1932. This school served children in the centre of town and later was used as a Rest Centre in the Second World War. The old school was demolished and replaced by a modern building with landscaped grounds instead of a yard and was opened in 1988. It was renamed Ramsden Infant's School in memory of the first mayor of Barrow.

St Paul's CE School was a church school and served families from the Hawcoat area. It was established in 1842 and was on the corner of Hawcoat Lane and Wheatclose Road. It has not been a school for many years; a new one was built further down Hawcoat Lane in 1957. The school building has been turned into halls and a community centre but has survived. The photo is of the pupils outside the school in 1929.

Victoria Junior School in Oxford Street was opened in 1884 and was originally for infants as well. This changed in 1917 when the new Infant School was opened higher up Oxford Street. This school survives as a working school and has outlived its contemporary buildings. The old Senior School behind the Infants has also gone. The Junior School was relocated to Devonshire Road in 1978 and the Senior School was repackaged and became part of the comprehensive system. The demolished schools are now housing, which seems to be the ultimate end for defunct schools.

Another school that has disappeared is Abbotsmead in Friars Lane. This was a large and unwieldy school that was difficult to heat and maintain. It was absorbed into the older Victorian school next door. The school is now known as Cambridge Street School and most of the Infants School has been demolished and eighteen houses are currently under construction.

There are other schools 'missing in action'; this is just a sample. It is indicative of the pace with which school buildings become unsuitable or obsolete and most are swept away with only a few being repurposed.

Thwaite Street School Christmas play, 1932.

School photo outside St Paul's, 1929.

Victoria Junior School, Oxford Street. (Courtesy of Barrow Archives)

Abbotsmead Infant School site and new houses.

5

Leisure

Barrow was not only about work; leisure and play in those brief hours away from the workplace were important too. Often leisure time was spent doing simple things like visiting the park or local beach, exploring the countryside and places like Piel Castle or Furness Abbey and of course sport was a popular pastime. The town has always been keen on both rugby and football and has produced sportsmen of a high calibre, some of whom performed in the national arena, such as Willie Horne or Emlyn Hughes. There are numerous playing fields in Barrow, but some have disappeared or been repurposed. One of these is 'Little Park', as it was known. This was located around the Yarlside Road and Belvedere Road area. In fact, the electricity substation is still named after it.

The Barrow Football Club had used the pitch initially following their move from Strawberry Ground, but it was very basic, and they moved again in 1909 – this time to Holker Street. Barrow Rugby, who played at Cavendish Park, moved to Little Park in 1914 because the ground had been requisitioned for the war effort. Their first match there was against Bramley and they won 31-2. Although the ground was 2 miles from

Yarlside Road is on the right where Little Park was.

town the club stayed on, using the Ship Inn as changing rooms for the players. They bought the land in 1920 from Lord Richard Cavendish and erected two stands, one of which would be transported to the new ground at Craven Park. It was a well-attended ground and they had a crowd of over 12,000 in 1923 in a Challenge Cup game against Oldham RLFC. The club continued here until 1931 when the rugby club departed for Craven Park, where it is today.

For a very short time it was transformed into a Speedway track and then a greyhound racing track until the ground finally closed in 1932. The site was demolished and left empty until the 1960s when new housing was built, connecting with the 1930s semi-detached houses in Yarlside Road.

The photograph of the two rugby players are Bill Burgess and Charlie Carr, who played for Barrow, and was taken in 1924 at Little Park; they were posing to celebrate their selection for the Australasia Tour. Bill Burgess was a pub landlord who kept the King's Arms, then the Ambrose and eventually the Washington.

Cavendish Park, which has already been mentioned, has had numerous changes too. It was used by Barrow Cricket Club at first and had two pitches. In 1875 Barrow Rugby played its first match there and continued to use the ground until 1914. A grandstand had been erected and the club had a crowd of 12,000 in 1908 for a game against Hunslet. This demonstrates how popular the game was and the following it had.

In recent years Cavendish Park has become a community hub and playing fields. A charity grant funded the improvement and refurbishment of the sports centre, and it continues as a facility for the public to use recreationally. A music festival was held there

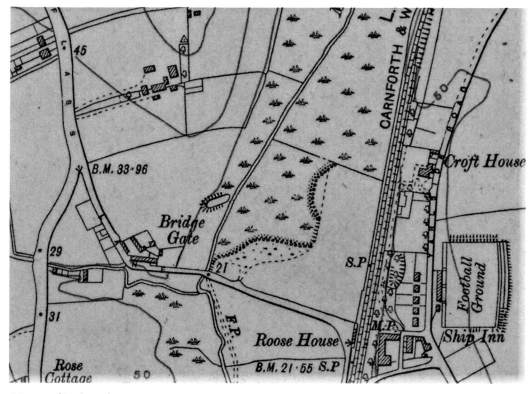

OS map of Little Park.

Bill Burgess and Charlie Carr.
(Courtesy of Keith Johnson)

Cavendish Park.

Community Centre at Cavendish Park.

last year in aid of charity and in memory of a local man, Richard Thorne, who sadly died of cancer. 'Fudstock', as it is known, was a great success and looks likely to continue for years to come, and Cavendish Park is a perfect venue.

Of course, sport is not the only leisure activity that Barrovians have enjoyed over the years. The geographical situation provides the town with beaches on every side of the peninsula. These have long been very popular with families and often in good summers they could spend a whole day there with little cost. The beaches are varied, some being sandy while others are covered in pebbles; they are all tidal and some can be very dangerous, especially on the Morecambe Bay side. However, since Victorian times townspeople have wandered their way to the beaches and have entertained themselves in very similar ways.

Generations of children have bathed, paddled and played in the sand and it is poignant to look back on the families through time seeing them enjoying themselves. Biggar Bank was always popular with people in town because it was within walking distance, or a short bus ride if you had the money. At the beginning there were not many amenities in Barrow, such as public parks, and people flocked to Biggar Bank. Ever-resourceful Walney farmers began to fence off the embankment and charge a small fee for access in the 1870s. This caused conflict and eventually the fences were removed and people were able to enjoy the countryside.

Barrow Council decided to lease the land in 1877 and made it open to the public. When the ferry was introduced across Walney Channel the footfall increased hugely. This led to purchase in 1881 and the council created a recreation ground for the town. The pavilions were added in which to purchase ice cream and refreshments and the area gained a traditional

Walney Beach and huts in the background.

Summer at Biggar Bank today.

Biggar Bank. Walney Island.

RELIABLE SERIES.

The Pavilion at Biggar.

'sea-side' feel. The Victorians had additional entertainments, such as Pierrot shows and other outdoor attractions.

With some disruption during the First World War the area continued afterwards to be developed into a small resort. By the 1920s and 1930s the popularity of Biggar Bank grew, and further amenities were introduced. There were swings and a playground and in 1931 an outdoor swimming pool was opened – in torrential rain! The pool was filled with seawater and it was unheated, but this did not deter the swimmers. It cost sixpence (around 2.5p) for adults and threepence for children (around 1.5p) to swim. For those who couldn't afford the pennies there was always the sea. The gang in the photo were on a day trip to the beach and were friends and neighbours in Manchester Street. The boy on the left next to the girl in a black costume is Sid Stockton. The boy beside the lad in plaid is Bill Cowan and the next but one is George Cowan in around 1936.

In 1957, a children's paddling pool was added, which became a major attraction, though many of us remember the grazes from the roughcast edges of the pool. Gala attractions were added too, as was the occasional beauty contest to select 'Miss Barrow'. The swimming pool was out of use by the mid-1960s and when harmful bacteria was found it had to close. The pool was demolished and filled in, leaving no trace except to the very observant. The paddling pool survived a little longer because this could be filled with chlorinated water, but that too was eventually filled in. A new children's play area has now been added in its place, but Biggar is a less exciting and resort-like proposal these days.

Other beaches like the Goadsbarrow, Roanhead and Askam provided simpler pastimes. These sandy beaches were ideal for paddling, picnics and playing. The ice-cream vans descended upon the most popular and these beaches were packed on sunny days. People still enjoy them, but perhaps there are wider opportunities on offer, which reduces the

Pierrots who performed at the parks and beaches.

Children from Manchester Street at Biggar Bank *c.* 1936.

Children's paddling pool in the 1950s.

Looking towards the site of the pools.

The Coast Road at Goadsbarrow in summer today.

number of beachgoers today. Of course, the beaches are subject to change, with erosion and new vegetation creeping in slowly and changing the environment, which is a loss of a sort.

An ever-popular outing was always the park. It was free, it was outdoors, and it offered various activities. Barrow Park is the largest park and famous because Thomas Mawson designed it; however, there were other smaller parks like James Dunn Park in Walney. The parks, although still there, have lost some of the entertainment that they once offered. The Pierrot troupes were often seen performing outdoors and of course there were opportunities to promenade and relax.

There were many different activities awaiting you such as boating, tennis, bowls and even at one time a children's petting zoo. The park has gone through numerous changes over the years and has developed according to need and fashion. The playground has been moved and is significantly safer than the earlier one, which had a concrete floor and a very high slide.

There is a new pavilion with community space and a small café, which is perfect for taking a break. The traditional pastimes are still there but there are new innovations too, such as the skate park and the miniature railway. A large portion of the 45-acre park was taken up by changing rooms and the Sports and Leisure Centre, and wide-open spaces that fronted onto Greengate Street have been greatly reduced. However, the park is still there and has adapted to meet the challenges of twenty-first-century living and has embraced some of the new ideas like the Parkrun, which is available every Saturday morning.

The park is keeping abreast of the times and has renewed the play park – a much safer experience these days than previously. So, although we have lost the quintessential Victorian park and some of the green space has been lost, there is a substantial amount remaining and the new innovations allow it to continue into the twenty-first century.

James Dunn park
at Vickerstown.

Public Park, Barrow-in-Furness

Barrow Park when
first constructed.

Looking towards
the renewed
bandstand in
Barrow Park.

Swimming has always been a popular pastime with young and old. The Barrow Swimming Baths on Abbey Road, built in 1914, gave children the opportunity to learn to swim and to take part in galas and displays. It was a relatively cheap entertainment and accessible to all. The baths had been severely damaged in 1941 during the bombing, but it survived and was repaired, and later extended in the 1950s. Many children were taken in school groups to learn to swim and gain their certificates and an abiding memory was the smell of chlorine and the taste of the minestrone soup after the lesson. The baths were sadly demolished in 1991 and replaced by the pool in the new leisure centre at the park.

Swimmers in Barrow Baths in 1934. (Courtesy of Barrow Archives)

6

Let Me Entertain You

Being a new town, Barrow attracted many workers. This in turn provided the opportunity for all kinds of entertainment to accommodate the masses. Much of this was cheap and cheerful, including the ever-popular music hall entertainments, theatre and later the cinema – rather grand ones too. Barrow now has only one multiplex cinema, situated on Hollywood Park. It is a popular venue and has a variety of screens available. In Barrow's early days, of course, there were many small cinemas and theatres, and some rather impressive ones. Some have survived the ravages of time and have been repurposed, others sadly have bitten the dust. The Electric Theatre in Buccleuch Street was in the 'cheap and cheerful' range and opened in 1910. Locally known as the 'Laugh and Scratch', it offered a 'full programme' no matter when you arrived. This would have been very popular and provided value for money. The programme changed on Mondays and Thursdays and would have shown all the popular films and shorts of the day. It was the first cinema to provide double seats for couples, presumably on the back row. It closed in 1957 and became a shop.

Many of these smaller theatres only had a short shelf life and were often converted for other uses. The Walney Theatre and Picture House in Natal Road on Walney opened in 1915 as part of the Vickerstown scheme and was sponsored by Vickers. This would allow Vickers employees living on the estate to access entertainment on the island instead of having to go into Barrow. It doubled as a variety theatre and later the local Operatic Society used it as their base. It was cheaper than the cinemas in Barrow, but the films were shown a week later. Eventually, they could not compete with the plusher and larger establishments and it closed, becoming a supermarket in 1964. It was later demolished and replaced with housing.

Another suburban cinema was built in 1920 in Salthouse. The Salthouse Pavilion in Roose Road has escaped demolition and is thriving in its third incarnation – this time as a church. It was another community cinema like the Walney Theatre but was slightly more luxurious. It had a small stage and a balcony, but the flaw in its design was that the seating was placed in direct lines rather than staggered. When it closed in 1959 it re-emerged as a new popular entertainment – bingo. This continued until recently when it was sold to Spring Mount Christian Fellowship in 2012. It retains its external features but has obviously been renovated inside to make it fit for purpose.

The Tivoli Music Hall in Forshaw Street was opened in 1868 as palace of varieties. These places were a popular form of mass entertainment and had acts ranging from quick change artists, singers, chair balancers and 'negro delineators' to name but a few. They were loud and rowdy with a rapid change of programme, with artists travelling from all over the country. In 1917, the theatre was taken over by James Brennan and films became more prevalent. In 1931, it became a proper cinema known as the Regal

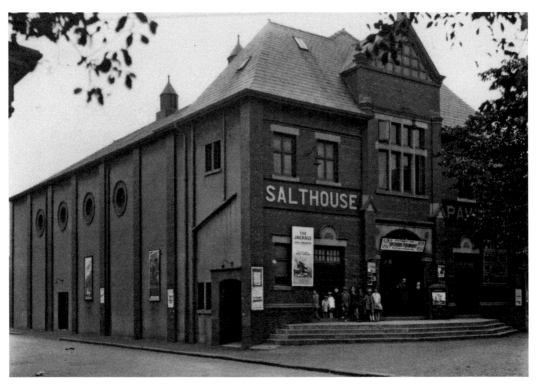

Salthouse Pavilion.

Regal Cinema.

Portland Walk.

and later in 1937 became part of Associated British Cinemas (ABC). It was not a warm or comfortable cinema and lost popularity, closing in 1956. The building was demolished in the 1980s and Forshaw Street is now underneath Portland Walk.

The Odeon, as many of us used to know it, traded under numerous names. Originally the Alhambra Theatre, it opened in 1872. It was slightly higher class than the music halls, presenting real theatre and music. It was rebuilt as the Royalty Theatre and Opera House in 1894 and sported an extended stage, trap doors, bridges and all the accoutrements needed for modern theatre production. It was ornate and modern with attention to the comfort of the performers as well as the audience. In 1937 the James Brennan Chain remodelled it, creating a state-of-the-art cinema. It was renamed the Roxy and opened with the Errol Flynn epic *The Charge of the Light Brigade*. It changed hands in 1943 and became the Odeon. Its final change was to the Classic in 1967. The author spent many happy hours here watching a range of films including Morecambe and Wise's *The Intelligence Men* (which went unfinished due to a power cut), Polanski's risqué *Macbeth* and 1970s romances like *The Way We Were*. It metamorphosised into the Champers nightclub in 1978 and Manhattan's in 1991. These, too, have fallen by the wayside and the building, though a dominant feature in Cavendish Street, is mostly unused and has a doubtful future going by the demise of others in the town.

Roxy Cinema, later the Odeon. (Courtesy of Barrow Archives)

Many older Barrow residents will recall the wonderful Her Majesty's Theatre in Albert Street. Its first incarnation was the ill-fated Theatre Royal, which opened in 1864. It collapsed during a storm and had to be rebuilt in 1868. In 1894, it was again rebuilt and emerged this time as The Empire, a variety theatre. This was an elaborate affair with a stall, dress circle, gallery and even two private boxes. It had some amazing acts in the real music hall tradition, such as troupes of lady dancers, Irish knockabouts and vocalists. It was the very first to show an animated picture in 1896 and continued as a music hall until it changed to His Majesty's in 1905 (later changed to Her Majesty's upon the coronation of Queen Elizabeth in 1953). Live theatre flourished here and by the 1940s it was being used as a repertory and variety theatre. It produced many notable plays including *Under Milk Wood, David Copperfield* and Lionel Bart's *Oliver*, which was an impressive new musical in the 1960s. It was demolished in 1972 and was superseded by the slightly characterless Forum 28, which never had the atmosphere and charm of the old theatre.

The Coliseum was an impressive building that dominated the corner of Rawlinson Street and Abbey Road. It might have been in disrepair, but it had a certain presence which sadly the small green and car park replacing it do not reflect. Originally a wooden construction called the Hippodrome, it was run by Calvert Routledge, who also ran the Empire. It was burnt down but was rebuilt

Forum Theatre.

and reopened in 1914 as the Coliseum. It was both a theatre and a cinema for many years and many will remember the excitement and fun of pantomime season as well as the place to see the newest films. Its doors closed in 1964 and finally succumbed to the demolition ball in 1977.

One much-lamented cinema was the Ritz, or ABC as it was known. This dominated the corner opposite to the Coliseum and was a fantastic art deco building, which met a worse fate than John Whinnerah Institute, which was in the same style. The building was a classic of its time. It was built in 1936 and had liveried staff, carpets, subtle lighting and a restaurant in its heyday. The features were typical, and it was a very exciting experience going to see a film, certainly during the war and after. It was taken over in 1977 and additional screens were installed. It variously became known as the Astra and then the Apollo. The picture house became obsolete in 1999 when the multiplex was built at Hollywood Park. It lay empty for some years and many suggestions were made to conserve it. However, a convenient fire gutted the structure in the early 2000s, rendering it impossible to develop. As often happens with empty buildings, vandals solved the problem, even though this building really should have been saved as a fine example of the art deco style. Its site has since been redeveloped (controversially) and the cinema replaced by a 'Marmite' building. Emlyn Hughes House is a modern

ABBEY ROAD, BARROW-IN-FURNESS

Putting on the Ritz – later the ABC Cinema.

edifice, as bold and structural as the art deco building it replaced. It makes a statement: mimicking the shape of a ship's prow, reflecting the town's marine history. However, many people fail to embrace its innovative style and decry it and muse over whether it is occupied or not. It is, Furness Building Society now occupy it, but there are still the deniers and decriers out there.

Opposite the Town Hall was The Palace Theatre, which was built in 1873 as the Royal Amphitheatre. In the 1890s The Palace was temporarily used by the Salvation Army until their citadel was built on Abbey Road in 1910. In 1912, the theatre was redesigned by George Walker and by 1915 it had 2,000 seats and was a cinema. It closed in 1930 for more modernisation and reopened as a cinema, presenting 'talkies'. The first picture shown was *Whoopee*, starring Eddie Cantor, in 1931 and it was under the management of James Brennan. It changed hands again, being taken over by national chains. Finally, in 1948 the Essoldo Circuit took The Palace over, running it until 1963 when it was transformed into a bingo hall. This continued until the 1990s when it was demolished to make way for the Wilkinson's store, which is still there today.

Abbey Road was the home for numerous picture houses, and the Gaiety Theatre and Picturedrome or Essoldo was yet another beautiful building. This was a cinema of epic proportions, a real picture palace of comfort and space built in 1913. The luxurious inside was special and it elevated the cinema visit to a grand night out. The entrance was approached by climbing imposing steps and then entering through beautiful decorated

Palace Theatre. (Courtesy of Barrow Archive)

Wilko's, where the Palace used to be.

glazed doors. There had initially been an orchestra to accompany the films during the silent era, but this was replaced by a Compton organ when the 'talkies' arrived. The first 'talkie', *On with the Show*, was shown in 1930 and from there it hosted many of the popular blockbusters like *Dumbo*, *Fantasia*, *Snow White*, *The Sound of Music* and the epic *Cleopatra*. It closed in 1968 and was later demolished. The building that replaced it is an uninspiring, block of functionality, known as Jubilee House.

Jubilee House, a poor replacement for the more attractive Essoldo.

7

Shopping

Shopping habits have changed – probably forever. The days of busy, shop-lined town centres are mostly gone, giving way to the homogenous supermarket or online shopping. This change has caused a doughnut effect in many towns and Barrow presents a sad and unloved aspect to the world. I write this as the news arrives that Marks & Spencer, established in Barrow in 1911, is to close in November 2019. This is one of the mainstays of the town at present and the worry is that it heralds further degeneration of the high street. The last large store remaining is Debenhams and we can only watch and wait to see if its fate is also sealed. Many of the national high street chains have disappeared from the main shopping street: Woolworths, of course, Saxone, Greenwoods, Freeman, Hardy Willis, Dewhursts and local businesses that no longer have a place such as Redman's, Bruccianis, Dolings and more.

The local Barrow Bid in conjunction with council and local businesses are desperately trying to regenerate the town, but the high cost of rates set by the government and the demographic changes in shoppers makes it a difficult task. Some of the side streets are thriving with small shops, which is encouraging, but one wonders what the impact of Marks and Spencer's closure will have upon them. So, it is no wonder that we look back so nostalgically at the old town and the myriad of shopping opportunities there once was.

One constant has been the Co-operative Society. Although the largest store, which was on the corner of Dalton Road and Abbey Road, has now become a Wetherspoon's pub and hotel, it had endured for many years as a store that had everything you might need. The Co-op in Barrow was established by men who worked for the Furness Railway in 1860. The first shop was in Greengate Street and was rented. This soon became too small and they purchased land at the corner of Mount Pleasant and School Street. The Dalton Road site was built in 1889 and became an emporium for every item under the sun. By 1960 the town had twenty-six grocery shops, known for fair prices and ethically sourced goods and of course the famous 'divi'.

However, the Co-op is still going strong in the suburbs, providing food and provisions as it always has. The Co-op in Roose Road has survived and recently underwent a renovation – a different aspect to that in the photo in 1937, which shows the 'assistants' in their white aprons. Doug Livingstone, Syd Williams (twenty-three) and John Pilkington are shown here. Dalton and Askam have retained their stores and there are a range of Co-ops across Barrow and Walney.

Some shops remained but changed hands. The Co-op at Yarlside became an independent shop and is now a Mace Store franchise. The structure of the shop is the same but on the other side of the road the two corner shops are gone. These shops were legendary: Arthurs sold everything known to man but had very strict proprietors, which

Early Dalton Road.

Marks & Spencer, Dalton Road. (Courtesy of Barrow Archives)

Shop assistants at Roose Road Co-op, 1937. (Courtesy of V. Vichich and P. Williams)

made sweet purchases risky, whereas Chapman's next door was less well stocked but had friendlier owners. Both shops were sold on. They have now become private houses and the new owners reclaimed the forecourts to make gardens.

Small shops were the order of the day when the town was new. Nearly every street had a corner shop – a convenience store packed with the necessities for life. Off-licenses too were part of the street scene. Frank and May Crane ran the off-licence in Westmorland Street from around 1962, when they first took it over. They had run pubs from the 1930s (Cumberland Arms in McLintock Street, right next to the rugby ground) and the Old Bay Horse, now Paul French Salon. They stayed in Westmorland Street until 1976 when Mrs Crane retired. Despite a long working life she lived until 2014, aged 102.

Roose village had a full range of shops, from a Co-op to a butcher's and a post office. There were corner shops too – Deans shop was next to the school and full of goodies to buy. The post office has been changed into a house, but retains its 'Post Office' name on the wall. The Co-op and butcher's changed several times but now there is only a small post office and shop, with the addition of a bank machine outside.

Roose Road Co-op.

Mace Store replaced the
Yarlside Co-op.

The houses where Arthur's and Chapman's corner shops once stood.

May and Frank Crane in their off-licence at Westmorland Street. (Courtesy of Ian Walmsley – their grandson)

The old Co-op and butcher's, now a post office at Roose.

The original Roose Post Office, now a house.

Specialist shops have almost disappeared. Hetherington's was a haberdashery shop – most people these days would not recognise this term, let alone understand what was sold there. Advertised in the 1934 Year Book, the range of goods was extensive – from umbrellas to fabrics, and from hosiery to quilts. In the days when people still made their own clothes these emporia were vital. In Barrow we were well served by the Trimming Shop (everything needlework related), Sterns for fabric and material and paper patterns, and of course the Wool Shop for all your knitting and crochet needs. With the advent of cheap imported clothes and people buying rather than making clothing, these shops have all but vanished. Those of us who can remember them do so with affection. The polished wooden counters, the smell of cloth and drapery, the colourful and eclectic mix of goods and the massive choice and range all contributed to a satisfying shopping experience.

Other specialist shops like Dolings, a good old-fashioned hardware shop, sold everything from buckets to waste bins. It managed to survive until very recently, moving from its Dalton Road premises to make way for Subway. Sadly, it too has gone, and we must resort to the uniformity and plasticity of the supermarket range of goods, which are nowhere near as inclusive.

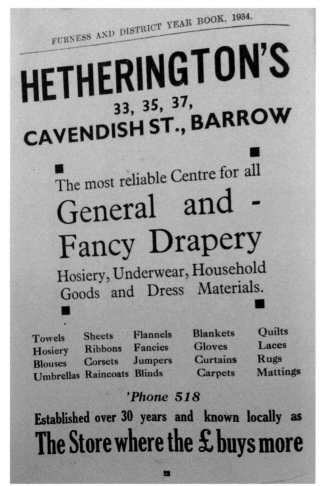

Advert from 1934 Year Book for Hetherington's Haberdasher.

Doling's hardware shop in Buccleuch Street.

Gaskins was a traditional cobbler based at the top of Dalton Road. The remaining shoe repairer in Barrow is Timpson's in Portland Walk, but it does not have the same use as the old shop. Gaskins was a busy place, where everyone had their shoes repaired. People valued good shoes and their longevity was extended by reheeling and soling. The smell and noise were unforgettable: glue and leather and the whine of the heavy machinery and tools. The finished goods, picked up later by presenting a paper receipt, were smartly wrapped in brown paper – no nasty plastic here and all very sustainable. At the top of Dalton Road was Rigg's shoe shop, where most children ended up having feet measured for school shoes in the 1950s. Next door is Browns the Busy Bee, where clothes for children could be bought – notable for its aerial receipt system on pulleys and wires. Across the road was one of the Italian ice-cream shops, Franchi. This was developed into a frozen food outlet later in the 1980s but is no longer on the high street.

Greenwoods and Frank Wood shops are worthy of note, the former a gentleman's outfitters with the more traditional attire of shirts, suits and overcoats. The place where you could buy cufflinks and trilbies. It never really moved with the times and perhaps therefore is why it finally closed recently; it has now become a trendy restaurant. Frank Wood was even more bespoke. It sold hats, gloves and masculine accessories. Presumably the hat trade is now in decline, unlike previous decades when a hat was an essential part of dress. When Forshaw Street was demolished to create Portland Walk

Rigg's shoe show and Browns The Busy Bee next door. (Courtesy of Barrow Archives)

Franchi's ice-cream shop. (Courtesy
of Barrow Archives)

Frank Wood hat shop.

this shop was removed and taken lock, stock and barrel to Beamish Museum where it has been recreated to endure in its eclectic and old-fashioned way forever.

Markets were an important part of the shopping scene from medieval times onwards. Although Barrow did not have a traditional market charter like Ulverston or Dalton it had a remarkable Victorian indoor and outdoor market – the brainchild of Sir James Ramsden. The market was a magnificent metal and glass construction, built in 1864 and taken over by the council in 1874. It housed a myriad of goods and sellers. Special sections were home to the fish market, the meat market and items like haberdashery. The outdoor market was busy and vibrant and there were small roundabouts for the children as well. The market was demolished along with Paxton Terrace and Paxton Street and the land reclaimed. The Public Hall remained for a time and behind the Town Hall a landscaped garden area was created and the inevitable car parking. The new market was opened by the Queen in 1971 and was a monumental concrete structure typical of 1970s architecture – ugly yet functional.

Some of the traders moved into the new market and continued to thrive. One such was 'Ted's stall', which sold fancy goods and household wares. Ted had been on the outdoor market until the move to the new building. Ted Price retired after twenty-six years of market trading in the new market hall. He was well known and well liked by his customers and was always friendly and pleasant.

The Public Hall was replaced by Forum 28 and these two buildings dominated the street in front of the Town Hall. The road was busy and bus stops were placed along it. The old Paxton Terrace was swept away, as was the taxi rank and other peripheral buildings. Much

Greenwoods, now a restaurant.

Barrow Market prior to demolition. (Courtesy of Barrow Archive)

Barrow Market, prior to demolition. (Courtesy of Barrow Archives)

Ted Price on his stall in Barrow Market. (Courtesy of S. Howell – Ted's daughter)

Ted's stall on the outdoor market before moving into the new market. (Courtesy of S. Howell)

Paxton Terrace was demolished to make way for the Civic Hall and market.

Building the Civic Hall and market complex.

later it was decided to create a one-way system and a pedestrianised plaza separating the two massive edifices. Unfortunately, the plaza is frequently a wind tunnel and not somewhere to loiter. The outdoor market is much diminished, relegated as it is behind the indoor market.

The Market Halls, however, have had a regeneration and house a vast range of stalls of all kinds, creating an energetic and eclectic shopping experience. Like all shopping in the town, there is a constant battle to drive shoppers towards this cornucopia of retail goods. It does seem to be having a resurgence in popularity and the management work hard to keep the experience fresh and attractive. However, Dalton Road is no longer the bustling shopping street it once was. We have explored the reasons for diminishing shops and shoppers, but one wonders if the pedestrianisation was the success it was hoped to be. The work was done and redone until it became what we see today. The shopping experience has diminished and although it is safer with no cars it has not really enhanced things. The gazebo in the photo has since been removed and repaving has taken place since the work in the 1990s.

Pedestrianisation in Dalton Road where it meets Cavendish Street.

8

Furness Abbey, Abbotswood and Furness Abbey Hotel

No book about 'lost' Barrow would be complete without mention of Furness Abbey. Naturally, the existence of the abbey is in evidence with the extensive ruins and its influence on the land has been covered previously in the chapter on rurality. It was the hub of the community, socially, religiously and through its administration of the land and property it held. The Cistercian overlords governed everything from fisheries to salt ponds and they meted out justice at the court in Dalton Castle; in fact, there was virtually no aspect of life that they did not influence or control. Their presence was sometimes paternalistic and at other times adversarial, but they shaped the land and the community, and we continue to observe these effects even today. We can see what has been lost, but we can't understand the real impact the abbey had because it is too

The chapter house where the Deed of Surrender was signed in 1537. (Courtesy of English Heritage)

distant; however, we can explore the more recent history connected with this important medieval site.

Following the dissolution, the abbey lands were carved up and sold off and the fabric and contents of the abbey plundered. The abbey was surrendered by Roger Pele and his monks on 9 April 1537 in the beautiful chapter house. The abbey had a poor reputation both locally and further afield by this time, mainly through constant misdemeanour and litigation by the monks, especially Abbot Alexander Banke. Many would not have been sorry to see it disestablished, but there were those who would become destitute and unprotected. One wonders how the monks with their meagre pensions fared and even more so those nine widows of the parish who were maintained by the abbey.

The new landowners utilised the building materials to build a manor house and the monastery became an unofficial builder's merchant, with local people taking stone and timber for their own use. Glass has been found as far away as Urswick, timbers at Broughton Beck and carved stones in many cottages and walls around the district. The dispersal must have been wide, and we are lucky to retain as much of the abbey church as we have. Scrolling forward to the nineteenth century the new owners had abandoned the manor house and were developing ideas to use the site for a different enterprise. The Furness Railway, owned by the Duke of Devonshire, carved a route alongside the abbey – much to the horror of celebrated poet William Wordsworth. Even today the trains rattle past the east window at great speed, separated only by the river and a few metres of grass.

This was the time of rail travel, which eventually blossomed into tourism. A new station and hotel were built on the site of the old manor house and it became a pivotal venue for the tourists of the day and was included in the tour of the Lake District. It had

The tunnel running through the abbey precinct.

been redesigned and converted into a hotel by Sharpe and Paley. It was later extended in 1866–69 and linked to the newly built station. It must have been a grand affair. Looking at the photographs, it had a veranda, a billiard room and a ballroom. The view was across the neatly trimmed lawns looking onto the abbey ruins. The station had a ticket office and a 'second-class' buffet – presumably for those who could not afford to dine at the hotel. This amazing building endured until it was demolished in 1954 and little is left to show it was ever there apart from the roof line against the back of the Abbey Tavern.

The Abbey Tavern was a public house until around 2007. It was a popular venue for socialising and meals out. Sadly, it went into decline and was empty for eight years until English Heritage bought it. Its future, although secure, is as yet undecided. It is a Grade II listed building and has some interesting architectural details, with some of the stonework from Furness Abbey being reused. One especially interesting, yet small, detail is a carved diamond-shaped brick, probably dating back to the Savigniac monastery. Locals love the building and await with great anticipation to see what will happen to this lost structure.

The abbey precinct is surrounded by interesting buildings; some of which are constructed from the lost stones from the abbey itself. One building which was lost in the flurry of 1960s demolition and rebuilding is Abbotswood, which was above both the railway station and hotel in the woods. This was the home of Sir James Ramsden and was a grand building suitable for his high estate. The Furness Railway leased it to him, and it passed to his son Frederic after his death. Fred produced no children and the building was given to the council who demolished it.

A nuclear bunker was built, but this too is now lost. The house is a sad loss, especially considering its link to Ramsden and the heritage of the town. Some of his possessions

Furness Abbey Hotel.

The now empty Abbey Tavern.

Abbotswood.

Archaeology in the woods from the Second World War.

and furniture are in the Town Hall and there are photographs of the house in its heyday. The grounds were separated into gardens, orchards and greenhouses and the archaeology is still there if one looks hard enough. The house was used during the Second World War for the military and there was an encampment in the woods. Again, remnants of the barracks are evident in the undergrowth. The woods are now a public green space, which is popular with local residents. There is a wildflower meadow and woodland paths and at the site of the house there is a grassed area for recreation.

The abbey area is an evocative place and much loved. It has had many events and re-enactments in the past and we regret that some of these will never be repeated. One of the most remembered are the mystery plays that were held inside the abbey. One wonders if this would pass the scrutiny of health and safety regulators now, but the photographs suggest not. These plays were presented from 1958 into the 1960s with a cast of at least a hundred. They ceased when it became difficult to recruit so many participants.

The 1961 event involved children from schools and local amateur dramatic societies and has reached a mythical status over the years. The photographs show the depiction of biblical stories recreated within the abbey walls, producing an authentic effect.

The plays were briefly revived in 1988 when illustrious celebrities became involved under the leadership of David Marcus. Peter Duncan of *Blue Peter* fame played Christ and the other parts were played by locals. Prince Edward famously visited Furness Abbey to see the plays and Melvyn Bragg also attended. The loss of these outdoor

Mystery play performance in 1961 at Furness Abbey. (Courtesy of Barrow Archives)

Precariously perched on the cemetery arch – no longer allowed. (Courtesy of Barrow Archives)

In the nave performing Bible stories. (Courtesy of Barrow Archives)

The holy family progression to Bethlehem. (Courtesy of Barrow Archives)

David Marcus (in blue), director of the Furness Abbey mystery plays in 1988.

Rehearsals in the abbey for the mystery plays, 1988.

theatrical events is much lamented, but it would be more difficult to put something of this magnitude on.

One final word about 'Lost' Barrow. We have retained many significant buildings and can glory in them, but many others have been lost due to neglect, arson or demolition. Some buildings like Abbotswood are irreplaceable and it seems counterintuitive to have demolished them and often the council is blamed, which it was indeed in this case. Frequently, however, buildings become too costly to maintain or bring up to date and are in private ownership. These often end up destroyed by fire and in the end demolished. Other buildings are part of the civic collection and again sustainability and the temptation of the developer's pound comes into play. The Grammar School buildings, although worthy and beautiful, were valued only by their land sale and as no other use could be found they were demolished. The picture to end with is of the House of Lords, the social club that Sir James Ramsden built. It was an attractive building and was historically important. Sadly, this too went the way of many others: the owner absent, the fabric in disrepair, the cost prohibitive and open to the vandals who burnt it down. This building was a Grade II listed, yet its status could not protect it. It is important therefore to monitor and value these old buildings before they are all sacrificed to modernity and are eradicated completely.

The derelict House of Lords – another one bites the dust.

Acknowledgements

As with most enterprises, compiling and writing a book such as this is not done in isolation, therefore I have many people to thank for their assistance. As usual Barrow Archives have been very helpful, especially Susan Benson, who shows great knowledge and patience and has been an invaluable support. Photos and information have come from many sources: the aforementioned archives, the Dock Museum, English Heritage and my personal collection of photographs and postcards. I would like to thank Susan Howarth, Valerie Vichich, Paul Williams, Keith Johnson and Ian Walmsley for the loan of their old photographs to use in this book.

Copyright materials have been used from Historic England, National Trust, Greenlane Archaeology, English Heritage and the Dock Museum.

I have used many pictures collected over the years and postcards by Tuck, Valentine, Real, Sankey, Atkinson and some family photographs. I have tried to ensure permission for copyright material has been sought. However, if I have inadvertently used any copyright material without permission or acknowledgement I apologise, and we will make the necessary correction at the first opportunity.

The following publications have been referred to during this research:

Barnes, F., *Barrow and District*
Beck, T., *Annales Furnessienses*
Greenlane Archaeology, No. 143 Salthouse Road, Barrow-in-Furness, Watching Brief
Leach, A., Collective Works
Trescatheric, B., Collective Works
West, T., *Antiquities of Furness*
The Diary of William Fisher, Occasional Paper No. 15 (1986)